ALBERT EINSTEIN,
ZEN MASTER

The top 54 sayings of a
modern-day Zen master

MATTHEW S. BARNES

© Matthew S. Barnes, 2020

ISBN: 9781706696803

All rights reserved. This book or any portion thereof may not be reproduced or used in any manner whatsoever without the express written permission of the publisher except for the use of brief quotations in a book review. Printed in the United States of America. First Printing, 2020

amazon.com/author/matthewbarnes

ALSO BY MATTHEW BARNES

1. **The Zen-nish Series:**
   (amazon.com/author/matthewbarnes)
   The Tao Te Ching 101
   Albert Einstein, Zen Master
   The Tao Te Ching 201
   Jesus Christ, Zen Master
2. **Ancient Egyptian Enlightenment Series:**
   (amazon.com/author/matthewbarnes)
   The Emerald Tablet 101
   The Hermetica 101
   The Kybalion 101
   Bhagavad Gita 101
3. **Investing Series (Zen-vesting)**
   (amazon.com/author/matthewbarnes)
   Investing 101
   Investing 201
4. **Novels**
   (amazon.com/author/msbarnes)
   Folie; (a creepy, psychological thriller)
   Meet Frank King (psychological thriller)

DEDICATION

For Donna B., my Zen master.

CONTENTS

Introduction ix
1 3
2 5
3 6
4 7
5 8
6 9
7 10
8 11
9 12
10 16
11 18
12 19
13 20
14 22
15 25
16 26
17 27
18 29
19 31
20 32
21 34
22 36
23 37
24 38
25 39

26	40
27	41
28	44
29	45
30	46
31	47
32	49
33	51
34	52
35	54
36	57
37	59
38	61
39	63
40	64
41	66
42	69
43	70
44	72
45	74
46	76
47	78
48	80
49	82
50	84
51	86
52	88
53	90
54	93
Consider Reading Next	95
Letter from the Author	97
Author Bio	99

INTRODUCTION

This book is meant to be fun. It's not meant to be a scholastic attempt at linking Albert Einstein to authentic Zen beliefs or teachings. Nor is it meant to be an exhaustive explanation of either Zen or Einstein. That being said, I did use Einstein's thoughts and quotes as an introduction to simple Zen concepts, as well as a few deeper Zen teachings.

How did the idea for this book come about?

As I was writing about Eastern philosophies and Eastern religions in other works, I would look for a quote to top each chapter off. On a regular basis, one of Einstein's quotes would come up that matched the subject. Eventually, I came to see a similarity between what Einstein and the Eastern philosophies were saying, and came to see Albert Einstein as a modern-day Zen master - in his own way.

What follows is a handful of Einstein's quotes followed by commentary linking his thoughts to my understanding of Zen. As in all my other works, I'm going for the "big picture". I'm trying to outline the forest, not get lost in the proverbial trees. In Einstein's own words, "Make everything as simple as possible, but not simpler." And, "If you can't explain something simply, you don't understand it well enough."

There is a tradition in speaking of Zen, usually by people who are not practitioners, to equate Zen with simply being "chill", laid back, or something similar. There is another tradition, usually put forth by beginners, of trying to make Zen sound as complicated, mystical and confusing as possible. I am not a fan of either of these approaches. For me, Zen *is* simple, but not flippant.

Einstein was a truly soulful man, yet he wasn't religious in the least, as he so adamantly claimed - at least not in the dogmatic way that most of us are used to. He believed in the miracle of life but didn't define it in the narrow viewpoints he felt each religion preferred and often demanded. What I hope to gain in this writing is to point out that a person can be spiritual, religious even, without fitting neatly into any particular religious or denominational category. In fact, I feel Einstein's understandings went *beyond* organized religious thought.

At one point, Einstein compared science to the study of an enormous clock that he called the universe. He said each scientist was viewing this immense, vast clock through a pinhole, doing his or her best to make sense of the clock given the extremely limited viewpoint with which it could be studied. This analogy can be applied to our attempts at understanding God - we're all trying to understand something that is vastly beyond us from the extremely limited viewpoint of our human minds.

Einstein didn't believe in a personal God. He believed that we, as people, like to give God names, give God motives and moods, give God favorites - but that is our doing. For Einstein, God and the universe are far beyond our ability as humans to understand. The best we can do is sit back and enjoy the miracle, studying it the best we can all the while. This understanding falls neatly in line with my perception of Zen, Taoist and Buddhist philosophies, just to name a few.

One more concept before we start: the Dunning-Kruger effect.

When I was in graduate school, I had a friend that was a straight-A student. Yet after each test, C and D students would argue with him about the answers he had chosen. The arguments often became heated. Even though my friend was prepared, the confidence of the other students would often cause him to question his own answers. This happened repeatedly.

When we got our scores back, even though my friend got an A and the other students got much lower scores, the other students still argued that they were correct. This always baffled me. Then I came across the Dunning-Kruger effect.

According to the Dunning-Kruger effect, people with lesser experience and a lower understanding of a subject tended to over-exaggerate the extent of their knowledge while those with more extensive knowledge of the subject tended to underestimate their understanding.

Here is how this effect was explained to me:

A novice photographer, just beginning, may see the field of photography in a very limited way. To them, there is not all that much to learn, and they have already learned quite a bit. Thus, they overestimate their abilities.

A professional photographer, on the other hand, who has been studying for years, sees the art of photography as a vast and never-ending field of study; so broad that he or she knows they can never hope to learn it all. Compared to how much there is to learn, the professional photographer doesn't feel they know all that much and therefore underestimates their abilities.

I see this same effect play out all the time. Regular citizens watch a single news source (one slanted to their liking) and feel they know all there is to know about politics. Religious adherents only read their Bible, and only the "good parts" at that, yet feel they know everything there is to know about God. I even see this law in effect in my clinic as a health-care provider. Patients come to me for help with a malady, yet often feel they know more than me and all my years of research and clinical experience because they read something once on the internet, or consulted "Dr. Google".

I think we all do this to a degree.

I have a family member that worked for the government. She was an "insider" when it came to the steps the government was taking to thwart another 911 incident. I once tried to ask her opinion on the progress of making flying safe after the terrorist attacks, but I had to give up. There were other people around her who kept butting in and answering for her, telling me what their news channel said was going on. There was an insider in our midst, one with in-depth knowledge of the situation, yet I couldn't find out her opinion because the people around her, much less educated on the subject, felt they already knew it all.

My point is that maybe Einstein was onto something. Maybe he was able to dive so deep into the mystery of this universe and the source of it that he was able to achieve a much more complex appreciation for it than most of us have the mental capacity for.

At one point, a "wise man" reportedly contacted the Oracle of Delphi. He asked the oracle who the wisest person in the world was. The oracle replied "Socrates".

Hearing the proclamation, disgruntled wise men from all over the area confronted Socrates, who was every bit as surprised by the oracle's announcement as they were.

After meeting with several of the wise men, Socrates claimed that perhaps the oracle was correct. He found the wise men to be full of themselves, thinking they knew all there was to know, while he was acutely aware of how much he didn't. Socrates felt life to be an endless, infinite quest for knowledge, a knowledge that humanity had barely dipped a single toe into.

"My wisdom," Socrates basically decided, "lies in my knowledge of how much I don't yet know. The wise men's ignorance, conversely, is rooted in their belief of how much they think they already do."

As W.B. Yeats put it, "The best lack all conviction, while the worst are full of passionate intensity."

As the Chinese put it, "Only the extremely wise and the extremely ignorant know all things." The Chinese parable goes on to say that few and rare are the extremely wise, though the world is full of the other.

It does seem to me that most people of this world are granted either intelligence or confidence, but rarely both.

Perhaps Uncle Albert was onto something. Perhaps he had an appreciation for the intelligence of the universe that we can't yet understand.

To get my points across, I'm going to use Zen masters, Buddhists, Taoists, and even a little Willy Wonka and Dr. Seuss. There are a lot of repeated ideas in the text that follows, but in a way that is a good thing. It takes a lot of repetition to understand ideas outside of what society is constantly throwing at us.

> *"We are the music makers,*
> *and we are the dreamers of dreams."*
> -Willy Wonka

1

"Reality is merely an illusion, albeit a very persistent one."

The first explanation that comes to mind in explaining the Zen of this quote is literal - the world *is* an optical illusion...

The world around us looks solid, yet everything we see is made up of atoms, which are, in turn, made up of energy. This world is *nothing* but energy vibrating at different speeds. Air and water vibrate at different speeds than wood and metal, giving them their different appearances of solidity.

As the world and everything in it is nothing but energy, it would seem that we should be able to walk through walls or push a twig of grass through metal, but we can't. The world is not solid, yet it is. Before us is an illusion - yet a stubborn one.

From the purely Zen perspective, we do not see the world as *it* is, but as *we* are. What we see is a kind of illusion, a filtered version of reality, not reality itself.

As a child, we see the world as it is. Then the people around us begin to pitch in; we see a shape and we're told that it's a "cat" or a "dog" or a "cow." If our parents or friends are prejudiced, they may tell us, "That's a Muslim (or a Christian, or a Jew), they are bad." And so on.

As we are taught *how* to see the world, our perceptions solidify into the reality of those around us. They *teach* us how to see what they see. Our egos form out of what we inherited genetically combined with this influence from those around us. It becomes a filter through which we view the world, not as it is, but as our filter perceives it.

Shake that ego, learn to see beyond it, and the world opens up to you as it actually is, not as our egos show it to us. In Zen, this is called "Awakening" or "Enlightenment", and is an experience beyond all that can be conveyed in words. We're then able to see that we are not our egos, but something more. And the world around us, likewise, turns out not to be what we thought it was, but something more as well.

*"I assure you that unless you
change and become like children,
you will never enter the Kingdom of heaven."*
-Matthew 18:3

2

"Great spirits have always encountered violent opposition from mediocre minds."

Ultimately, for me, this quote goes back to the Dunning-Kruger effect I spoke about in the introduction...

The more learned a person is, the deeper his or her understanding of a subject is, the more appreciation and respect that person tends to have for the subject. Great minds are open to exploring possibilities other than those that are currently known.

The less educated a person is, on the other hand, the shallower his or her understanding of the subject, the more basic the subject seems to be. They believe there is no more to learn. This leads to strong, outspoken opinions and a closed mind. These types of people are very resistant to change - afraid of it. They want the world to fit into their understanding. It's the only way they feel safe. The world must stay flat, so to speak, for them to sleep at night, and they will fight with all they have to keep it that way. Familiar. Safe.

"The universe must not be narrowed down to the limit of our understanding, but our understanding must be stretched and enlarged to take in the image of the universe as it is discovered."
-Sir Francis Bacon

3

*"I have no special talents.
I am only passionately curious."*

The prerequisite of learning is an open mind...
Once, a student came to a famous Zen master. It was the third Zen master the student had contacted.

The Zen master sat the student down to interview him. Every time the Zen master tried to explain the aim or goal of his teachings, or what to expect, the student would interrupt: "That's not how we did it at the last school," he would say, or "Yeah, we did that too at the last school. Only we did it this way or that way."

Unable to get a good word in, the Zen master began pouring tea for the two of them. But when he filled the student's glass, he ran the tea to the top, then let it flow over.

"Stop!" the student yelled. "Can't you see that the cup is full?"

"And so is your mind," the Zen master said. "There is no room for anything else in there."

Those that know it all have no room for more, yet there is always more to learn.

"No more will go in."
-Nan-in

4

*"Two things are infinite:
the universe and human stupidity.
And I'm not sure about the Universe."*

Not his nicest quote, but many Zen masters of the past were known for being sharp with their tongues.

Not to beat a dead horse, but this quote goes well with the last one. Stupidity isn't a lack of knowledge but the illusion of it - an ailment that seemingly affects a large portion of society.

Believing you already know everything prevents further growth.

*"The greatest enemy of knowledge is not ignorance,
it is the illusion of knowledge."*
-Stephen Hawking

5

"If you can't explain it simply, you don't understand it well enough."

There is a tendency for people to try and sound like they know more than they do. They (we) often use big words to make up for in expression what they (we) lack in comprehension. Most of us have this problem. It is especially evident in Zen.

Bankei, a famous Zen master, reportedly obtained a deep enlightenment. Afterward, he traveled the area, seeking other Zen masters to see if anyone had reached a level deeper than his own, hoping to study with them.

After questioning these masters on subjects only an enlightened person would understand, Bankei found that most of them had not attained enlightenment at all, and they admitted it.

The teachers claimed that they inherited their Master's disciples and had to play the part, so they simply quoted their late Master.

*"If you can't dazzle them with brilliance,
baffle them with bull."*
-W.C. Fields

8

"Everyone is a genius. But if you judge a fish on its ability to climb a tree, it will live its whole life believing that it is stupid."

This one is pretty much self-explanatory - we are all smart in some ways, talented in some ways, yet not so much in others. I, for example, can solve puzzles like a madman but can get lost in my own house.

Society tends to value one talent or aspect of genius over another, yet what society values changes with the times. At one point, doctors were lowly servants. Now, they are highly thought of. At another point, martial artists held great status, now they are more of a novelty.

We are all talented in our own way, whether it is "in" right now or not. Yet we tend to view the value of another human being based on how respected their particular talent is by the current viewpoint.

From a Zen or a Buddhist perspective, all beings have "Buddha Consciousness" or "Christ Consciousness". All beings contain "the Unborn", as Zen Master Bankei would say. Call it "Soul" if you like. We are equal, just different.

"Every man I meet is my superior in some way."
-Ralph Waldo Emerson

9

*"Education is not the learning of facts,
but the training of the mind to think."*
&
*"The only thing that interferes
with my learning is my education."*

If a person memorizes facts, they are limited to current knowledge.

To go beyond this, you must strive not only to learn what is already known but to also explore and think for yourself so that you can break new ground.

There is a parable that is prominent in the physics community. According to this parable, a professor was asked to be a referee on the grading of an examination by one of his colleagues.

The colleague was about to give his student a zero for his answer to a physics question whereas the student believed he should get full credit. The question was: Show how it is possible to determine the height of a tall building with the aid of a barometer.

The student's answer was: "Take the barometer to the top of the building, tie a long rope to it, lower the barometer to the ground, mark how far the rope had traveled, then bring it back up. Measure how much rope it took to reach the ground and you have the height of the building."

The student argued that he had given a perfectly correct answer to the question. The teacher argued that the student had not demonstrated a knowledge of physics in his answer, which was the point of the examination. He couldn't give him an A in physics when he had shown no understanding of its principles.

The professor suggested the student have another shot at answering the question. Both the teacher and the student agreed.

The student had six minutes to answer the question in a way that would show some sign of his understanding of physics. At the end of five minutes, he hadn't written anything. The professor asked if he wanted to give up. The student said no. He said he had many answers to this question, he was just trying to figure out the best one to give. In the last remaining minute, he quickly jotted out his favorite answer: Take the barometer to the top of the building and lean over the edge. Drop the barometer and time its fall with a stopwatch. Knowing the weight of the barometer and the time it takes to reach the ground, you can then calculate the height of the building.

At this point, the professor asked his colleague if he would like to give up. He conceded, giving the student almost full credit.

In leaving the office, the professor remembered that the student had said he had many other solutions, he had just picked his favorite one. So the professor asked him what the other answers were.

The student answered that there were a great many answers to the question. For example, you could take the barometer out on a sunny day and measure the height of the barometer and the length of its shadow. Then measure the length of the shadow of the building. Using simple calculations of proportion, you could then easily determine the height of the building.

The professor agreed, then asked for others.

The student offered a basic version. He said that you could take the barometer and begin walking up the stairs of the building. As you climb the stairs, you mark off the length of the barometer along the wall. Knowing the height of the barometer, you could then count the number of marks on the wall to come up with the answer.

The student then offered a few more sophisticated methods, using pendulum swings and the like.

The student concluded with what he felt to be the best method: Take the barometer to the basement and knock on the superintendent's door. When the superintendent answers, tell him you have a fine barometer. If he will tell you the height of the building, you promise to give him the barometer.

At this point, the professor asked the student if he really didn't know the conventional answer to the question, the one his colleague was after.

The student admitted that he knew the answer and gave it to them, but said he was fed up with instructors trying to get him to conform to what was known instead of seeking out new ways. Telling him what to think instead of how to think.

The student turned out to be Niels Bohr, a Danish physicist who made tremendous contributions to the understanding of atoms and quantum theory.

Later scholars feel the story is not factual but a parable teaching the importance of creative thinking, not rote memorization.

In either event, it promotes Einstein's idea here: Learn to think for yourself so that you can go beyond that which is already known.

A proverb says: "Give a man a fish and they eat for a day; teach a man to fish and you feed him for a lifetime."

The scientist would say: "Give a man a fact and their knowledge will be current; teach a man to think and he'll make new discoveries."

The Zen master might say: "Teach a man what you see and he'll confirm your view of reality; teach him to see for himself and he'll be free."

"Do not seek to walk in the footsteps of the wise.
Seek what they sought."
-Matsuo Basho

10

"Insanity: doing the same thing over and over and expecting different results."

&

"We cannot solve our problems with the same thinking we used when we created them."

Above are two more self-explanatory quotes: If you do the same thing, you get the same result. It's as simple as that.

There's a book called *Strange Life of Ivan Osokin* by P.D. Ouspensky, written in 1915.

The story takes place in Russia and follows the life of an unhappy youth, Ivan, who has just said goodbye to the love of his life. *If only I had a chance to go back and relive my life up to this point,* he thinks, *then it would all be different.*

He's given the chance by a mystical Magician who sends Ivan back to his childhood at the orphanage when everything started going wrong.

But Ivan finds it almost impossible to go down a different path, to make different choices, to choose different actions, and ends up in the same predicament.

The Magician informs Ivan that this wasn't his first attempt at changing his past. Not his second either. Evidently, the Magician had sent Ivan back countless times, only for him to end up in the same predicament each time.

Life is mechanical, the Magician tries to tell him, and the laws of this world are absolute, immutable. Make the same choices and you end up, over and over and over, no matter how many times you try, with the same result.

The only way to break out of the loop is to break beyond the knee-jerk reactions of the ego (my Zen explanation) and begin to make informed, conscientious choices. For *things* to be different, *you* have to be different.

This fits neatly into Zen thought.

As a side note, Harold Ramis, who directed *Groundhog Day*, found the meaning of this novel to be very similar to the existential dilemma of *Groundhog Day*. Ramis' opinion is printed in the Lindisfarne Books' 2004 edition of *Strange Life of Ivan Osokin*.

For things to change, you have to change.
For things to be different, you have to be different."
-John Rhon

11

"Only one who devotes himself to a cause with his whole strength and soul can be a true master. For this reason, mastery demands all of a person."

According to Zen (and certain Buddhist practices), everything you do should be done with complete focus.

Whether doing laundry, meditating or driving, your full attention should be on the task at hand, not listening to the endless chatter of your mind.

The path to enlightenment, say the masters, is as thin as a razor's edge. Stray even the slightest bit to the left or the right and you've lost the path.

"Do or do not, there is no try."
-Yoda

12

"A person who never made a mistake never tried anything new."

The point of life, according to enlightenment theory, is to grow in consciousness; to mature in awareness beyond the level of mind we are currently at so that we can expand to a much higher level of being.

In order to do so, you must push forward, try new things, strikeout, then try again. It's the very definition of growth.

Yet we fear failure and ridicule, and so remain on our iceberg, wishing there was a way off.

Ego is restricting our expansion, our destiny. It fears non-existence, yet we give it the only existence it has.

There *is* a way off the iceberg, you just have to find it.

And to find it, you'll have to try things you've never tried before, or else you will keep getting the results you have always gotten.

"A ship is safe in the harbor,
but that's not what ships are made for."
-William Shedd

13

"I live in a solitude which is painful in youth, but delicious in the years of maturity."

According to Zen and similar philosophies, life is a gradual maturing of consciousness.

As a child, we believed in Santa. We also believed that we could get into the cake we weren't supposed to eat, get it all over us, and still deny we had any. It made sense at the time.

As we age though, our consciousness matures and what seemed so obvious before now becomes ridiculous in retrospect.

I for one look back at my teen years and early twenties and wonder how I survived. I was self-centered, cocky and dense.

As we age, our mind matures and we develop understandings that we never had before. According to Chinese Taoist theories, boys tend to have mental leaps every 8 years, while females follow 7-year cycles. In other words, females start to question the magic of Santa and similar beliefs around age 7, while for boys it tends to be around 8. Boy's switch gears again around 16, while for girls it's around 14.

The point is that as we age our brains mature and our level of consciousness rises. We begin to be aware of things we had not been aware of before, and start to understand concepts we had struggled within our youth.

We lose the desire for the loud music of our younger days, the parties on the weekends, and so on, and begin to develop a taste for the subtle. For the quiet and mundane.

As simple and natural as this sounds, it is a sign of spiritual progression. The point of Zen and other similar teachings is simply to speed up the natural maturation process. When the mind progresses to a certain point, it transcends this world. The goal is to do so now, before the death of the body, not after.

"Let silence take you to the core of life."
-Rumi

14

*"I never teach my pupils.
I only attempt to provide the
conditions in which they can learn."*

This idea falls fully in line with Zen training for me, furthering my belief in Einstein as a modern-day Zen master.

In today's society, we are all taught *what* to think, not how to think for ourselves. In Zen training, it is exactly the opposite.

If you were told by your Zen master *what* to think or believe, you would still not be thinking for yourself, only replacing society's beliefs with your Zen master's - not your own. Instead, with Zen, you are given the tools to reach the desired destination yourself.

To become infatuated with anyone's teachings or beliefs instead of seeking to obtain reality for yourself is famously punished in Zen. For example, a student who idolized the Buddha was told by his Zen master that the Buddha's teachings were "shit on a stick" - the equivalent to modern-day toilet paper. Did the Zen master not like the Buddha? No. The point is to find reality for yourself, not to get sidetracked by idolizing the Buddha or his teachings - something many religions seem to do. Our religious leaders have pointed to the path we need to walk, yet we are notorious for becoming fixated on their pointing fingers, missing the path they are trying to guide us onto. We worship the leader instead of following the path.

Zen masters have developed several unique techniques to guide their students beyond the chattering of their own minds (egos) and into the realm of objective reality - question and answer sessions with masters, meditation practice, mindfulness training, and probably most famous, the Zen koan.

What follows is my understanding of the Zen koan:

There are three levels of mind: subconscious, conscious and superconscious. I define the conscious mind as mostly our egos, which have been trained by society around us into a very specific and agreed-upon view of reality. The koan is a riddle ingeniously designed to be unanswerable by the conscious mind as we know it.

The koan is designed to exhaust the analytical, intellectual, egotistical conscious mind so that the superconscious mind can have the space it needs to break through. It is a sword designed to cut the intellectual mind to shreds so that something higher can emerge. It is a blender used to shatter the fixed thinking of the subjective mind to clear the route to intuition and imagination. This higher level of mind, referred to by other religions and philosophies as the soul, surpasses the intellectual realm and takes you into the realm of simply knowing. It is an intuitive level of mind where there is no struggle to understand - understanding simply emerges on its own.

Ever think so hard you finally give up, only to have the answer emerge on its own later? This is the intuitive, superconscious mind leaking through when the conscious mind has been exhausted. The koan is a tool for doing this intentionally.

We're all looking for answers - why are we here? Is there a God? Is there a Heaven? Does life go on? But we are using our limited, analytical, egotistical, intellectual minds in the quest. As Rumi once noted: "Maybe you are searching among the branches for what only appears at the roots."

Here is a famous Zen koan: When both hands are clapped a sound is produced; listen to the sound of one hand clapping." There are many others, and worth looking up if you are interested.

"Out of nowhere, the mind comes forth."
-The Diamond Sutra

15

"Not everything that counts can be counted, and not everything that can be counted counts."

There is a level of reality that exists beyond our senses. A level that bleeds into our current level and is the most important part. Love, compassion, and wisdom are examples. These things exist and are actually the most important aspects, yet they cannot be counted as you can count money or possessions. Living from the point of view only of that which can be seen and counted is the very definition of misery. Living from the other aspects is the only path towards peace.

The world is a living entity. Imagine it as a great clock or a great city, churning on endlessly. Viewed from afar (from the viewpoint of the subconscious mind), the clock is beautiful, the city splendid. Immersed in the day-to-day activities of life within that clock or within that city (viewed from the ego, the conscious mind), you are going to get caught up in the wheels from time to time. You are going to be a victim of pollution and thievery and drama. It's nothing personal, you are simply caught up in the cogs of life.

To be happy, you must find a way to rise above, where the view is spectacular.

"Let go or be dragged."
-Zen Proverb

16

"Learn from yesterday, live for today, hope for tomorrow. The important thing is to not stop questioning."

As a repeat of the last chapter, life is a living entity, churning on in endless cycles. For the most part, you can't control what comes - the good or the bad. You are not in control. Life is.

Some things *are* in our control, like being nice to each other, furthering our education, and so on, but overall, life is simply life living out its own cycles. Good things are going to happen and bad things are going to happen. Sometimes the tornado will miss your house, sometimes it won't. Sometimes you and your loved ones will live long, productive lives. Sometimes those lives will be harsh, maybe even cut short. It's nothing personal. It's just life living itself out, just like you are living your own life, unaware of the bacteria and cells of your bodies that are living and dying, experiencing both good luck and bad, wars and peace.

The only way to lose is to quit trying.

"If we are facing in the right direction, all we have to do is keep on walking."
-Zen Proverb

17

"The true sign of intelligence is not knowledge but imagination."
&
"Logic will take you from A to B. Imagination will take you everywhere."

These two quotes are similar to Chapter Seven's quote, *"Imagination is more important than knowledge. For knowledge is limited to all we now know and understand, while imagination embraces the entire world and all there ever will be to know and understand."*

I listed the two quotes above separately because I wanted to make a different point.

The egotistical, intellectual mind is limited to those things that can be seen, analyzed and counted. It is limited to the viewpoint of the conscious mind, which has been shackled by the ego and the opinions of society.

The superconscious, objective mind can see further. It can take you into a realm beyond that of the intellect. It is a realm of pure potential, and its mode of operation is imagination and intuition, not intellectual analysis.

Intellectual analysis has its place. It makes living more comfortable (air conditioning, heat, the internet, etc.). But it can only take you so far. Beyond its abilities lies a living world of endless possibilities, and from there do we draw the intangible inspirations that makes life *worth* living.

> *"There is no life I know to compare with pure imagination. Living there you'll be free if you truly wish to be."*
> -Willy Wonka

18

*"Try not to become a man of success,
but rather try to become a man of value."*

In Zen, we are told to set about our daily tasks with all the zeal of our souls. Whatever it is that we are doing, whether as frivolous as counting clouds or as serious as open-heart surgery, we are to do it with full attention.

Tom Cruise noted this very thing In *The Last Samurai,* when his character, Nathan Algren, went to live with the Samurai. He says, "They are an intriguing people. From the moment they wake, they devote themselves to the perfection of whatever they pursue." He noted that the villagers that were having tea were every bit as devoted to the task at hand as the Samurai who were practicing their skills in the fields.

What is the reward? Money? Success? That may come. The person who does a job extremely well will always have an advantage over the one that does not. Try for money or success without value though, and it will not last.

That being said, the reward is greater still: the act itself is the reward. Doing a good job is the reward. A man who creates success without creating value is an unhappy man. The man who creates value though, whether rewarded financially or not, finds it easy to sleep at night.

Further, by perfecting whatever task we are performing, the mind cannot wander to the past or the future. It stays here and now, ⟨in the living moment,⟩ where it is safe and at peace.

> *"Set thy heart upon thy work,*
> *but never on its reward."*
> -The Bhagavad Gita (Hindu Bible)

19

"Play is the highest form of research."

To tap into the full potential of the mind we must move past the egotistical, analytical thinking mind into a realm that exists beyond - the realm of intuition and imagination we have talked about before. It is in this realm that <u>imagination and intuition provide answers our thinking minds can't access</u>

You can't get there by thinking, but there are other ways. Play is one of those ways.

> *"A little nonsense now and then is relished by the wisest men."*
> -Willy Wonka

20

"Only a life lived for others is worthwhile."

We as a species are self-centered. We are even taught to be this way. Many of our self-help gurus and therapists speak to great length about putting yourself and your wants and needs and desires first. Yet those who have found the greatest happiness in this world are those who have found their way beyond the ego-centric viewpoints of life, and their teachings are very different.

"Life is so very difficult," Buddha once said, "How can we be anything but kind." He also said, "Helping one person may not change the world, but it could change the world for that person."

Albert Schweitzer, the celebrated physician and humanitarian, once said, "One thing I know: the ones among you who will be really happy are those who have sought and found how to serve."

"Intense love," says Mother Teresa, "does not measure. It just gives." She also said that "The hunger for love is much more difficult to remove than the hunger for bread."

We're all in this thing called life together. We're all lonely and scared. Those among us who seem to be the happiest are those who look beyond themselves and their own dramas in order to give the most, not the least."

Buddha once said, "Give, if only you have a little." And also, "If you knew what I know about the power of giving, you would not let a single meal pass without sharing it in some way." And, "No one has ever become poor by giving."

> *"Thousands of candles can be lit by a single candle,
> and the life of the candle will not be shortened.
> Happiness never decreases by being shared."*
> -Buddha

21

"The intuitive mind is a sacred gift and the rational mind a faithful servant. We have created a society that honors the servant and has forgotten the gift."

The superconscious mind is the seeming void from which new ideas and possibilities originate. These ideas come to us in dreams and during times of relaxation, and we say, "the idea just came to me out of the blue."

The conscious mind is what takes those new possibilities and finds a way to bring them to fruition in our world.

The idea for the internet, for example, came from the imagination. The intellectual mind solidified it into reality. Same with all new ideas and inventions.

The conscious mind knows only what is, not what can be. It is a tool for bringing dreams to reality. The superconscious mind is the well from which these dreams emerge.

The intellectual mind is therefore meant to be the *sidekick* of the superconscious mind, yet, for most of us, is the one and only viewpoint through which we experience this world. It is what we live from.

I am repeating myself, but to move beyond the world as we know it and begin to live from an entirely different realm, the superconscious mind must be brought to the forefront. We all have insights that originate spontaneously from the superconscious mind. The practice of Zen is aimed at bringing it forth intentionally and permanently.

The emergence of the superconscious mind is referred to in Zen as "Enlightenment" or "Awakening."

A seeker asked the Buddha, "Are you a God?"
The Buddha answered, "No,"
"Are you an angel?"
Still, the answer was, "No."
"Are you a healer?"
"No."
"Are you a saint?"
"No."
"Are you the messiah?"
"No."
"Are you a teacher?"
"No."
"Then what are you?" the exasperated student wanted to know.
"I am awake," the Buddha replied.

22

"The woman who follows the crowd will usually go no further than the crowd. The woman who walks alone is likely to find herself in places no one has ever been before."

Zen is a very simple practice, but one that needs repeating in order to be understood.

Once again, in my opinion, Einstein was saying the same thing that we have been going over, just in a different way.

The conscious mind chains us to what is known, what is accepted.

In order to find a different path, you have to leave the path you are on.

It's a difficult undertaking, walking a different path than the one you are used to, the path society is used to, but the rewards are what make it worth the while.

Two roads diverged in a wood, and I—
I took the one less traveled by,
And that has made all the difference.
-Robert Frost

23

"The strange thing about growing old is that the intimate identification with the here and now is slowly lost; one feels transported into infinity, more or less alone, no longer in hope or fear, only observing."

As we age, we begin, over time, to lose our self-importance. We begin to feel a separation from the link we had at one time been so addicted to with our bodies and our egos. We begin to feel less attached to this world.

Not everyone matures in this manner at the same rate, but the wisest among us talk frequently about the phenomenon. Perhaps they have reached a level of understanding that others often do not.

The intent of Zen is to speed up the process. To reach that level of existence here and now so that we may view the wonderful city from afar, so-to-speak, completely free of the drama of living within its walls. There is no more fear. No more frantic hopes or dreams for money and success and love that spur the ego into emotion, only a detached, peaceful observation.

"Those who do not move do not notice their chains."
-Rosa Luxemburg

24

"If people are good only because they fear punishment, and hope for reward, then we are a sorry lot indeed."

Einstein was not a fan of mainstream religion. Especially Western religion.

The Hindus, Buddhists, Taoists, and others taught us that we should do what is right because it is the right thing to do, not because it will get us something we want. If you are only doing what your religion tells you is right out of fear of punishment or the hope of a reward, then your intent is not true. Your behavior is coerced, not genuine.

Ultimately, giving makes us happy, we just get so caught up in our own wants and needs and fears that we think we have to run over our neighbor to get what we want. This is ego-centered living.

> *"If this is going to be a Christian nation that does not help the poor, either we have to pretend that Jesus was just as selfish as we are, or we've got to acknowledge that He commanded us to love the poor and serve the needy without condition and then admit that we just don't want to do it."*
> -Stephen Colbert

25

"Life is like riding a bicycle. To keep your balance you must keep moving."

Life is like walking a tightrope. Look left and you'll fall. Look right and you'll fall. Look down and you'll fall. Quit moving and you'll fall. The only way across is by looking ahead and moving forward.

Life *is* movement. Anything that stops stagnates, dies.

Stagnant water is a swamp. Stagnant air is fetid. A stagnant body grows ill and a stagnant mind grows stale.

Keep moving.

"When you reach the top, keep climbing."
-Zen Proverb

26

"Few are those who see with their own eyes and feel with their own hearts."

Our minds have been trained from birth to accept society's vantage point of reality. It's hard to break free from that training. It's even harder to walk off from the crowd's point-of-view. It means isolation and, more often than not, ridicule.

The majority of us, therefore, live life through society's ideas, not our own. See reality through the eyes of the masses. And so we live in their reality - a life filled with angst and uncertainty.

Those few who do break free become the religious, spiritual and artistic leaders of our time. They trudge beyond the known world and try to lead us into the dreams of the future.

"All that we are is the result of what we have thought. What we think we become."
-Buddha

27

"In the middle of difficulty lies opportunity."

This explanation is going to go a little deeper into Zen philosophy. I am going to do my best with it.

First, a simple, surface explanation is that when you are faced with a difficulty, with a barrier, it is a chance to study something you have not yet come up against. Something you didn't know existed. It is a chance to study that barrier and figure out how to overcome it. As you do, your grasp of this world is broadened. You have removed a shackle you didn't even know existed, freeing yourself to take one more step forward. You have mastered one more aspect to life - you have moved past it.

In Zen, there is this idea of concentric circles. Around yourself is a circle. A little wider circle encompasses your family. An even wider one encompasses your friends, then your race, then your creed, then your nationality, and so on. Within the innermost rings are those things that are most like yourself, and therefore most familiar and acceptable. In the outermost rings are those peoples and aspects of life that are the most different from ourselves, and therefore most frightening.

As we grow and mature, we begin to break through wider and wider circles to become more comfortable with aspects of life that seem more foreign, scarier. The first time a telephone rings, it may terrify an infant. But with experience, the infant grows past that concentric ring - it becomes a part of its comfort zone. This happens over and over in life. The first hair cut is no fun at all. The first kiss is terrifying. The first job is horrific, and so on.

In the beginning, our circle of acceptance is very small, but as we mature, we begin bursting through layer after layer after layer. Every time we burst through the next circle, the one after that comes right up to us. The new circle before us is our next challenge at growth.

Here's where the philosophy gets a bit deep:

A student once told his Zen master, "You have to help me. I'm miserable. I can't take any more. Life's not for me. Please help me or I am going to die. Or at least I want to. I really do."

"First of all," the Zen master replied, "the peace you seek is nothing anyone else can give you. My experiences and beliefs won't do you a bit of good. Nobody's will. You could memorize every holy word ever spoken, yet it will do you no good. You have to reach the destination you seek by your own effort. It's a path we all take on our own. A path we must all complete on our own.

"Secondly," the Zen master went on, "within your suffering itself is the key to your liberation. It is staring you right in the face. The obstacle is the answer."

This is what the Zen master, at least in my opinion, meant:

What is it that is suffering? Was *the student* suffering? No, it was the student's ego that was suffering, his conscious, analytical mind. The ego is an illusion that doesn't even exist. It is a fictitious entity that is confined within and bound to the beliefs of this world. An entity that the student had taken to be who and what he was. It is the barrier the student had reached, the obstacle in his path to freedom."

So, according to the Zen master, the crisis itself had brought the student face to face with the answer that was needed. The problem was also the solution.

"I teach one thing and one thing only:" taught the Buddha. "Suffering and the end of suffering."

"The obstacle is the path."
-Zen Proverb

28

"The only source of knowledge is experience."

In order to truly know something, you must experience it for yourself:

If you want to know about tractors, you can't have someone simply explain them to you.

If you want to know about children, you have to raise a few.

If you want to understand love, you can't rely on hearsay.

And if you want to know about the reality of this world, you have to experience it for yourself.

"Training is useful but there is no substitute for experience."
-Lotte Lenya

29

"Only those who attempt the absurd can achieve the impossible."

Most people are confined to and by the analytical, intellectual conscious mind. Yet this constraint keeps them locked into the realm of that which is already known. The only things they can fathom are those things that already fit neatly into the possibilities the world currently knows.

Only those who are able to break through the educational training of society are able to reach beyond the known and into the realm of undreamt-of possibilities.

In 1875, a young Max Planck was advised by Philipp von Jolly not to study physics since "there was nothing left to be discovered in it".

Max Planck ignored the advice and eventually discovered energy quanta, which won him the Nobel Prize in Physics in 1918.

"Argue for your limitations and sure enough, they're yours."
-Richard Bach

30

"Any intelligent fool can make things bigger and more complex. It takes a touch of genius and a lot of courage to move in the opposite direction."

According to Zen, reality is so complicated that it's simple. The answer is staring you right in the face and always has been.

Those that don't understand it like to use big words and complex philosophies. Those that have experienced it find it simple beyond words.

"Sometimes the questions are complicated and the answers are simple."
-Dr. Seuss

31

"Any man who can drive safely while kissing a pretty girl is simply not giving the kiss the attention it deserves."

I'm going to explain this with a Zen parable:

"Once there was a man traveling across a field who encounters a tiger. He ran, of course, and the tiger chased.

Coming to a precipice, the man caught hold of the root of a wild vine and swung himself down over the edge. The tiger sniffed at him from above. The man looked to the ground below him only to see there was another tiger, waiting to eat him if he fell. Only the vine kept him from falling.

Two mice started to gnaw away at the vine.

The man saw a luscious strawberry near him. Holding the vine with one hand, he plucked the strawberry with the other.

How sweet it tasted!"

Reality exists here and now, in the present. The past is gone, the future is not yet here. In order to tap into the mysterious spark of life that animates this living world, you have to give your full attention to the present moment. You must experience it fully.

"If you are depressed," says Lao Tzu, "you are living in the past. If you are anxious, you are living in the future. If you are at peace, you are living in the present."

Your focus is your reality.

"Realize deeply that the present moment is all that you have."
-Eckart Tolle

32

"I do not believe in a person God and I have never denied this but have expressed it clearly. If something is in me which can be called religious then it is the unbounded admiration for the structure of the world so far as our science can reveal it."

Einstein was very direct and very specific about his religious beliefs. He did not believe in God in the Western religious sense of a human-like figure that lived in the clouds and showered favors on his favorites while punishing those he did not like. *the Web*

Instead, Einstein believed in an intelligence that makes the stars shine and the planets circle the sun in mathematical precision. An intelligence that makes galaxies and universes and souls. God was this intelligence for him, and it was measurable, observable.

No matter how much we love flowers, they die. No matter how much we dislike weeds, they grow. Being a good person is no guarantee of an easy life. The sun shines equally on both sinners and saints, democrats and republicans, the religious and the atheist. The world is run by an intelligence that created the laws by which it functions, not the moods of a fickle and human-like God. Belief or faith is no substitute for direct experience with this intelligence.

In Zen, there are no beliefs, no adoration for teachings or teachers, only the peace that comes from direct experience with the infinite.

"Zen Buddhism is a discipline where belief isn't necessary."
-David Sylvian

33

"There are only two ways to live your life. One is as though nothing is a miracle. The other is as though everything is a miracle."

Life is a miracle. The very fact that we exist and live and breathe and move is a miracle. As far as we have gotten with science, we still don't understand the spark of life that animates all that exists in this living world. Where does this spark come from before birth? Where does it go to after death? What exactly is this spark? Is it energy? Soul?

But it's easy to miss it, as ironic as that sounds. We get so caught up in our daily lives - drug into the past, pushed into the future - that we very rarely exist in the present moment where the miracle of life is playing out constantly before us; every second of every day.

Part of Zen training is learning to stay in the present moment. To be a witness to the miracle as it dances out before you. Stay long enough in the present and the miracle comes clearer and clearer into view, eventually blooming fully.

It is a very difficult task, except during childhood, where we lived in the moment.

Einstein's childlike enthusiasm for science seems to be what made his mind so amenable to the miracles before him - it kept him in the present moment, dazzled by what he saw.

"Don't wait for miracles. Your whole life is a miracle."
-Albert Einstein

34

"Creativity is intelligence having fun."

This quote sounds so childishly Zen-like for me that it's hard not to imagine Einstein in monk's robes while saying it.

We tend to equate superior intelligence with a serious demeanor. We look at the great minds of the past as stuffy old intellectuals that didn't know how to have fun. They had grim looks on their faces. They walked stiffly erect. They were quiet, stern. But the greatest among us have often been quite the opposite. Mozart used to gleefully send letters to his female cousin Basle describing his latest flatulence and the foods that caused them. He had such a "potty mouth" (the term historians have used) that there is a debate on whether he had Tourette Syndrome, a neurological disorder that causes outbursts of obscenities. The stuffy intellectuals are convinced he must have had the neurological disorder while historians feel differently. Often our greatest thinkers and most talented scientists have had a playful, almost frivolous and childish outlook on life.

Benjamin Franklin, another "gentleman" who was portrayed to us in school as a stuffy academic wrote a book called "Fart Proudly". In one of the book's stories called "Who's the Ass?", Franklin described a scenario with an old man, his grandson, and a donkey. The old man was trying to take his donkey to town to fetch some supplies and his grandson wanted to go along. On the way, every person he met had a different idea as to who, if anybody, should ride the donkey. Who's the ass? According to the story, you are if you care what people think. Everybody has their own, unique idea about how you should be living your life - and they are all convinced that they are correct. You just can't make everybody happy.

There is a story where a child was looking at a fountain. Beside him was a sweet, gray-haired old man who was also watching the fountain, but between his fingers. He was fanning his hand before him and looking at the fountain through his moving fingers. He showed the child how to do it. Upon trying it, the child found it created snap-shots of the fountain where it seemed like he could see pictures of the individual water droplets. The old man turned out to be Einstein.

Pablo Picasso fathered children with different women well into old age. Zen masters performed zany, hilarious tricks on their students.

It seems that many of those at the very top of the intelligence pole were not dogmatic intellectuals as we were led to believe, but playful, creative geniuses. Their vast talents and superior intellects seem to be rooted in a zeal for life that lead them into the world of imagination, which they found to be far superior to the world of simple intellect. True intelligence, at least for many of the most intelligent people in history, is not necessarily stuffy; it is playful, childlike, irreverent, regardless of how the greatest minds of our past are portrayed in the history books.

"It's never too late to have a happy childhood."
-Tom Robbins

35

*"True religion is real living;
living with all one's soul,
with all one's goodness and righteousness."*

This is a major concept in Zen Buddhism.
True religion, according to Zen Buddhism, is not found in belief or rote memorization of scriptures. It's not found in prayer either, where one is asking to be saved. Instead, it's found in saving ourselves; in walking the path for ourselves. It's found in what we do and how deeply we seek and find and walk the path. It doesn't matter how many scriptures we can quote, it matters only how well we live the life the scriptures are trying to lead us to. The reward is found in the path itself and no other place.

Zen Buddhists believe this was Christ's message as well, but Christians eventually worshipped the messenger instead of walking the path he was showing us. We made him our savior, our salvation, instead of living as he lived and tried to teach us to live.

True religion, Zen Buddhism teaches, is found in the correct living of life itself. According to Zen, we must put all we have into everything we do. In the very doing does the universe open up to us. Not doing for a reward, but doing because the doing itself is the reward. It takes us to the present moment where the constant, insistent chattering of our egotistical minds quieten and we move beyond the intellectual, analytical, self-centered mind. The danger is only here, in our current level of mind. Suffering is not caused by what happens, but in our mind's resistance to what happens; our mind's interpretation of what has happened. But beyond this level of mind is another level, one that gives us the safety and comfort we all seek. It is the God, the Heaven we all seek, and we can find it right here, right now. Once found, our troubles cease to exist.

Stay in the present moment and the miracle of life comes into view. The living intelligence behind it all comes forth and we can live within it. Stay in the present long enough and the mind "awakens" permanently to that which is beyond this level. Do this and we move permanently beyond suffering. Is this easy? Not at all. Our own minds are very hard to get past.

Further, being good because we fear punishment or seek reward is an equally false path. We should do good because it's the right path. Goodness is what our souls are made of. It's what our souls want. Living righteously ignites the happiness of our soul and is another path to the source. Helping others and living rightly does not lead to a reward; it *is* the reward. One that becomes more and more permanent the more we use it.

Once, the Buddha was asked about God and Heaven. Do they exist? What are they like? Buddha responded that if he described God or if he described Heaven, the people would miss the boat - later generations would argue with each other over what he meant in his descriptions instead of trying to find the path he was attempting to show them. The people would worship him and his words instead of walking the path for themselves. Instead, he said he was giving us the path to experience God and Heaven for ourselves. Once experienced, then we can describe it all to him if we want. He said that he was nothing, that he deserved no reverence. It was what was within him, what was within us all that deserved the reverence. We just didn't know how to get to it. He said he was simply showing us the path. He was the messenger, not the prize.

I believe Einstein found the present moment in his pursuit of science. The soul of the world opened up before him in his studies, and he lived within it. We each have our own path.

> *"No one saves us but ourselves. No one can and no one may. We ourselves must walk the path."*
> \- Buddha

36

"The value of achievement lies in the achieving."

This one goes back to the last chapter and is another major teaching of Zen, as well as Buddhism and Hinduism.

The value of achievement is found in the achievement itself, not in the promise of any kind of return or reward.

This teaching is felt to be true on many levels. First, the doing, in and of itself, is a reward. It makes us feel good about our accomplishment. I remember working construction during the summer of my college years. I loved going by houses I helped build or worked on and seeing what had been done. It gave me a sense of pride.

Secondly, we don't have any control over others. We don't have any control over what other people think or do. We can't control whether they like or appreciate us or our work. The only thing we have control over is ourselves: what *we* think; what *we* do; how proud we are of our accomplishments; how proud we are of how we have lived.

Lastly (though I'm sure there are others), throwing yourself into whatever you are doing lands you in the present moment. Done correctly, thoroughly, with all your soul, it brings you into "the now", where the miracle of life exists. As such, it is a tool for moving beyond the egotistical mind. It is a tool for touching the living, infinite world staring you right in the face. It is a tool for removing the blinders so that you may see it.

> *"In the end, people will judge you anyway, so don't live your life impressing others, live your life impressing yourself."*
> -Buddha

37

"Intellectual growth should commence at birth and cease only at death."

Even though, according to Zen, enlightenment is the goal, there is actually no end. It is spoken of as a final destination, but according to those that have awakened, the mystery continues on.

Famous Zen masters like Bankei spoke of increasing levels of enlightenment. After his initial awakening, Bankei spoke of continued learning, continued seeking of other Zen masters to deepen and further his enlightenment.

Though enlightenment is the goal, there are different levels, and no matter how far you get, there are always more levels.

The same can be said of any pursuit, including science. Gaining a degree can be compared to initial enlightenment, but this world is full of wonder. No matter how far we progress in the study of our chosen field, further discoveries are being made daily. Look at where we are now compared to just 15 or 20 years ago. Electronics have come a long way. So has medicine. Nearly everything has.

This world and all within it is a living mystery and one in which there is no final acquisition of knowledge, only a path that keeps extending out before us.

Those, like Einstein, that have seen it most clearly, have found that happiness lies in the continued pursuit. A pursuit that never ends. The only way to stop growing is to quit seeking, to quit learning. No matter how far you get, if you want to be happy, keep going.

As the Zen proverb goes, "When you reach the top, keep climbing."

"The unexamined life is not worth living."
-Socrates

38

"I have repeatedly said that in my opinion, the idea of a personal God is a childlike one. You may call me agnostic, but I do not share the crusading spirit of the professional atheist whose fervor is mostly due to a painful act of liberation from the fetters of religious indoctrination received in youth. I prefer an attitude of humility corresponding to the weakness of our intellectual understanding of nature and our own being."

&

"I cannot imagine a God who rewards and punishes the objects of his creation, whose purposes are modeled after our own — a God, in short, who is but a reflection of human frailty."

Atheists, according to Einstein, are often crusaders fighting against the intense religious indoctrination they received in their youth. Like these crusaders, Einstein has found the beliefs of a personal God that caters to its favorites and punishes its non-believers to be a childish notion. A God who is given the worst characteristics of a human being - jealousy and favoritism and egotism.

However, he does not agree with the atheists in their dismissal of any superior intelligence behind this living world. Call him an agnostic if you want for his lack of belief in a personal God, but he did not see himself as an atheist.

For Einstein, religion is the humble acknowledgment that the human race has barely scratched the surface in understanding the living reality of the world before us. Heck, we barely understand our own being. He stood in humble awe before the mystery of this life. In that way was he religious.

This is very much the way that Zen and Zen Buddhist masters describe what they have experienced during enlightenment. They describe a living intelligence, miraculous beyond what can be conceived in our current level of mind, but chuckle at the idea of this intelligence being personified; given all the shortcomings and erratic emotions of human beings. This intelligence, they say, is beyond the motivations and understandings of the human race.

Once we enter the infinite, unified mind, say the Zen masters, we see and think as it does. And what you see and how you think surpasses the motivations of the human mind.

Thomas Edison also said, "I have never seen the slightest scientific proof of the religious ideas of heaven and hell, of future life for individuals, or of a personal God."

> *"He who experiences the unity of life sees his own Self in all beings, and all beings in his own Self, and looks on everything with an impartial eye."*
> -Buddha

39

"Energy cannot be created or destroyed, it can only be changed from one form to another."

This quote shows another way in which Einstein's teachings can be compared to religious thought. Einstein was portraying with his findings in science a common teaching found in most religious texts - we are all immortal. Everything is immortal.

At the essence of all living beings, and even inanimate matter, is atoms. Atoms are made of energy, and energy can neither be created nor destroyed. It can only change form.

Zen Buddhists say the same thing about our souls. Namely that they can neither be created nor destroyed, but can only change from one form to another.

Buddhists believe in reincarnation. They believe that even our souls are made of energy. Energy that gets recycled into other beings at our death.

Who knows?

The point is that, even according to the laws of science, this world, at its source, is nothing but energy. And that energy can neither be created or destroyed. It can only change forms.

"The world is afflicted by death and decay.
But the wise do not grieve,
having realized the nature of the world."
-Buddha

40

"Concerning matter, we have been all wrong. What we have called matter is energy, whose vibration has been so lowered as to be perceptible to the senses. There is no matter."

&

"It followed from the special theory of relativity that mass and energy are both but different manifestations of the same thing."

These are two more quotes on the reality of the universe from Einstein's scientific point of view that agrees with a point of view that has been promoted since ancient times by those that have awakened.

This world may seem solid, but it's not. It is nothing but energy vibrating at different speeds. The speed of vibration determines how solid the object appears to us. The more solid an object appears, the slower the energy it is made of is vibrating. The less solid an object appears, the faster the energy it is made of is vibrating.

At the slowest vibrational levels, we get things like rock and metal - very solid objects. At faster rates, we get water and smoke and steam - relatively non-solid objects. But at the highest rates, we get phenomenon we can neither see, smell or taste. X-rays, for example, and gamma rays. There are other phenomena vibrating at even faster rates than can't even be detected with the best scientific equipment we currently have.

At the highest rates of vibration, we find consciousness itself, which is the root, the source of this world. Consciousness is thinking all else into existence. And it didn't do it just once. It is still doing it now, every second of every day.

This universal consciousness, according to Zen masters, is what you are trying to tap in to and live from. And the only way to find it is to move beyond the chattering egotistical mind of your lower self and into the great, unified mind.

"There is no matter as such - mind is the matrix of all matter."
-Max Planck

41

"The religion of the future will be a cosmic religion. It should transcend a personal God and avoid dogmas and theology. Covering both natural and the spiritual, it should be based on a religious sense arising from the experience of all things, natural and spiritual as a meaningful unity."

Einstein, as noted before, was very critical of what he believed was a "childish" view of religion. He believed in a much more mature and nuanced understanding of the power that animates the living world.

He felt religion transcends a personal, personified God. He felt religion should go beyond dogma and theology, beliefs that have been forced upon non-believers, often at the point of a spear or the barrel of a rifle. He also felt that most organized religions fell far short of the admiration we should have for all aspects of the miracle of life.

For many believers who don't consider themselves to be religious, most organized religions are not spiritual. I have personally been around extremely religious people who have littered, treated animals badly, turned their backs on the poor and even make fun of mentally challenged people.

A family member of mine was at a church function when a homeless man knocked on the kitchen door. He asked if he could come in and warm up (it was winter) and have a little food. This family member told the man he didn't have the authority to make that decision, but that he'd ask the minister, who he was sure would say yes. But the minister said no. He told my family member to give the man directions to the homeless shelter, which was several blocks away. Later, while eating, the minister said he couldn't wait to die and meet Jesus to see how pleased he was with him.

I have also directly experienced needy people being ignored by the congregation of one church after another. The congregations volunteered quickly for car washing and other fundraisers where their good deeds would be seen but remained silent when people with Multiple Sclerosis and Lou Gehrig's Disease pleaded for help.

There is an old joke where a colored janitor in a white church in the south asked the minister if he could sit in the congregation just this once, since it was the Christmas service. He had never asked before. The minister said no. The old janitor sat alone and cried. Jesus suddenly appeared before him and asked why he was crying. "They won't let me pray with them," the janitor explained. "I wouldn't worry about that," Jesus replied, "I've been trying to get in for years myself, and they won't let me in either." Substitute the black janitor with a gay or poor janitor and it's the same concept.

This disconnect between goodness and spirituality with dogmatic religion seems to be lost, more often than not, with the dogmatically religious. They don't see what littering, treating animals badly, turning their backs on the needy and making fun of the mentally ill have to do with the teachings of the Bible. I personally think Jesus would disagree. They seem to think religion is showing up to church, having faith that Jesus' actions make up for their own, singing loudly and converting others to their religion. Nothing more.

According to Zen Buddhism, goodness is goodness. It is written on each of our souls. Our souls are created from it.

We act kindly because it is right, not because it is written in a book. Religion, for them, is the totality of how we live, not restricted to teachings from a book.

Further, Zen believes in experience. Religion isn't something you memorize or recite but something you come in contact with for yourself through your own goodness. Religion is coming in contact with universal consciousness, which is goodness, love itself.

Religion is something to be experienced, understood, not memorized. And it encompasses the totality of the way we live our lives.

> *"Religion is rather the attempt to express the complete reality of goodness though every aspect of our being."*
> -F.H. Bradley

42

"The more I study science, the more I believe in God."

Once again, Einstein is proclaiming his belief. Just not in the manner of a personalized God whose theology has been narrowed into an analytical dogma.

Einstein's religion was experiential. He found, through the study of science, proof of an intelligence at work that is beyond human intellect. He stood humbly in awe of this power.

For him, religion wasn't a theory to be obtained from a book and debated over by different sects of admirers, each with their own beliefs, but instead, an actual experience that transcended all the writings in all the books ever written.

Zen practice is very much the same. It is based on an actual experience with the infinite instead of a theoretical belief in it.

> *"Any meditation practice or spiritual journey boils down to finding the answer to this great question, "Who am I?" As a practice aiming toward attainment rather than mere understanding, Zen does not rely on concepts, beliefs, theology or ideology. Zen's method is to evoke our own direct experience of life."*
> -Dae Kwang

43

"The most beautiful thing we can experience is the mysterious. It is the source of all true art and science. Whoever does not know it and can no longer wonder, no longer marvel, is as good as dead, and his eyes are dimmed. It was the experience of mystery that engendered religion. A knowledge of the existence of something we cannot penetrate, our perceptions of the profoundest reason and the most radiant beauty, which only in their most primitive forms are accessible to our minds. It is this knowledge and this emotion that constitute true religiosity. In this sense, and only in this sense, I am a deeply religious man."

Einstein is yet again testifying to the wonder of life that he has found through his studies. He has actually experienced something beyond the mundane. He has contacted it and it has changed him, giving him a sense of wonder and excitement he has a hard time putting into words. He can only say that it is there, and comparing his life before finding it to his life now is like comparing a living man to one that might as well be dead.

This concept falls easily in line with what the Zen masters have said in trying to explain the wonderment of enlightenment. It can't be explained, only pointed to, and once you see, it is as if you were not truly alive before.

This, to Einstein, is true religion. Not living with your eyes dimmed to what is right before you. Not looking forward to a future prize that exists beyond this world. It is studying the living miracle before you that eventually opens you up to its presence.

> *"The real meaning of enlightenment is to gaze with undimmed eyes ... "*
> -Nikos Kazantzakis

44

"I see a pattern, but my imagination cannot picture the maker of that pattern. I see a clock, but I cannot envision the clockmaker. The human mind is unable to conceive of the four dimensions, so how can it conceive of a God, before whom a thousand years and a thousand dimensions are as one?"

Zen Master Bankei's enlightenment occurred when, after a long period of meditation, he became sick. He couldn't make it any further. He couldn't see how to get there. His body was about to collapse and his mind, now exhausted, quit. He then spat on a wall and the sight of his blood-streaked saliva struck a chord. He saw. He knew. He was awake.

Many Zen masters describe similar experiences: intense concentration to the point that the egotistical mind fell away, exhausted, and then a mundane occurrence took them over the precipice.

I remember reading about one such master, though his name escapes me, who suffered so much that he decided to quit. He stopped meditating and laid on the floor. He imagined he was already dead. He wished he was already dead. He couldn't go on. He laid in the same spot for days on end, eventually wondering if he were actually dead or not. He couldn't tell. At some point, he even stopped thinking about that. It made no difference to him now. And so his mind quit churning and reality emerged.

This quote by Einstein reminds me of a Zen master describing his ascension into understanding. Einstein had all the facts in front of him. He knew the science. He knew the laws of this world and had great admiration for them. But in trying to envision the intelligence beyond it all, he ran into a barrier that couldn't be passed. Not by the conscious mind. Whatever that intelligence was, it was impossible by human understanding to come to terms with it. His mind churned, hit the wall and quit. Then the reality emerged. Not from the conscious mind, for it's not capable, but by the unified mind. The intuitive, unified consciousness beyond our ego-driven analytical minds.

"Silence isn't empty. It's full of answers."
-Zen Proverb

45

*"Science without religion is lame.
Religion without science is blind."*

In the beginning, according to Chinese philosophy, there was nothing but a oneness; a unified mind or energy.

In order to create and explore, the oneness split into two equal but opposite parts - the yin and the yang, which we can view as the negative and positive energies of the universe.

The negative energies coalesce to form negative particles called electrons. The positive energies coalesce to form positive particles called protons. The positive and negative particles clump together in endless variations to form atoms, which go on to form all the matter of the universe.

In our everyday world, yin is female while yang is male. Like electrons and protons, female and male come together to form more life forms.

What I am getting at is that this world, according to Chinese philosophy, is dual. What we came from is one, but what we have in this world is dualistic, divided. And it is very much human nature to pick one side and one side only. Men and women both think they are right. Democrats and Republicans think likewise. The same goes for men of science and men of faith.

Yet, ultimately, there is no right or wrong, just left and right, up and down, back and forth, male and female...two sides of a single coin.

Science is the study of life, religion is the appreciation for it. Science on its own is cold and dark. It contains just cold, hard facts. Religion by itself can be childish, ignorant.

Combine the two and the sum is greater than the two parts.

In Zen, there is much reference to moving beyond the dualistic, subjective, ego-driven mind. Beyond that mind is an objective, unified mind. One that is not split into yin and yang, left and right, high and low, right and wrong. It simply is.

"Out beyond the ideas of wrongdoing and rightdoing," says Rumi, addressing the duality, "there is a field. I'll meet you there. When the soul lies down in that grass, the world is too full to talk about."

For Einstein, the study of life and the appreciation for it are not in conflict. They are one and the same.

"I have put duality away.
I have seen the two worlds are one."
                  -Rumi

46

"God does not play dice with the Universe."

According to physicist Vasant Natarajan, "Einstein, of course, believed in mathematical laws of nature, so his idea of a God was at best someone who formulated the laws and then left the universe alone to evolve according to these laws."

Like the Buddhists, Taoists and Zen masters, Einstein sees God as the intelligence that created the world around us and set it up with laws of existence. Yet for them, God is not separate from these laws - God is both the laws and the maker of the laws, the designer and the design.

Western religion tends to view God as an entity that takes an active role in purposely moving life in a certain direction, specifically to favor his followers and to punish his non-believers. For them, this is purpose.

For Einstein and the Eastern religions and philosophies, God created life and made the rules. When bad things happen, it is not due to an angry, wrathful and jealous God, but due to your own error in living against the rules set forth. Eat poisoned, uncooked meat and you get sick. Go out in the snow naked and the same result may occur. Try to catch a falling tree and you get hurt, not because God is angry, but because you violated the laws of this world.

Life, according to Einstein is ruled by law. It is not random, it is precise, intentional. It's just not personal.

God exists, but not as a wish-granting genie. There is no judgment, only consequences.

> *"God causes it to rain on both flowers and weeds, sinners and saints, democrats and republicans, gays and straights. The laws are precise, but not personal."*
> -Me

47

"I want to know God's thoughts; the rest are details."

This quote is extremely Zen for me.

According to Zen teachings, we try to understand the details of life so that we may better understand God, but the way (the path) to awakening is the opposite: let go of your analytical, intellectual, egotistical conscious mind in order to find God.

This doesn't mean that you don't need the conscious mind. It's what helps us to survive in this world. We need to know that snakes bite, cold can freeze us and fire can burn us. It's the mind we have been given as a tool in order to better navigate and survive in this world. But if your pursuit leads to a knowledge of what is beyond this world, we have to use a different mind. The conscious mind is made for this world, the unified mind is of the next.

In order to tap into the unified mind beyond this dualistic world, we must trick our current mind into letting go so that we can see past it. As of right now, the ego-mind is in our way, blocking our perception of what is beyond it. Once you do move past the conscious mind, you gain an intuitive understanding not only of the next world but of this one as well, since you have tapped into the creative mind behind the formation and running of this world. You have tapped into the thoughts of God, the creator.

Enter the unified mind and the rest is nothing but details.

> *"If we find the answer (the unified theory), it would be the ultimate triumph of human reason - for we would know the mind of God."*
> -Stephen Hawking

48

"I am a deeply religious nonbeliever- this is a somewhat new kind of religion."

Most people (especially in the west) have a very specific definition of a religious person: It is an individual who believes in a higher power that is personified into a great human being, complete with our human motivations and emotions. The goal of life is to please that being in order to avoid punishment and receive rewards. Eternal life in paradise is one of those rewards.

I have a friend that I love dearly who exemplifies this belief. She was in tears of joy because she went to a Christian play called "Judgement House" where a bunch of high school kids had been killed in an automobile accident. The kids who had not yet accepted Christ as their Lord and Savior went to a burning Hell for all of eternity even though they were very good people. They had good hearts and had spent a lot of time helping others. The kids that had been saved, even though some of them were not very good people, all went to Heaven. They had accepted Jesus as their Savior. She found this extremely reassuring.

Einstein considered himself religious, but not by that strict definition. He had an overwhelming awe and reverence for life and the power that created and runs it. He simply didn't believe in a personified version of that power.

He felt that this would be viewed as somewhat of a new religion for most people. One they wouldn't understand.

Again, this viewpoint of Einstein's fits in nicely with the Zen teachings. *Experiencing* the divine was mandatory. It was nothing another could give you or do for you. And once obtained, true experiential faith began, not one that was based on memorizing scripture or saying that you believed in a higher power.

By society's definition, Einstein was a non-believer. Yet he was a believer, in his own way. And deeply so.

*"You should never doubt
what nobody is sure about."*
-Willy Wonka

49

"When you are courting a nice girl, an hour seems like a second. When you sit on a red-hot cinder, a second seems like an hour. That's relativity."

Time in our current understanding is dualistic and linear. It's split up into a before and an after, a now and a then, a past, a present, and a future. Our minds perceive events to be lined up in a nice procession, where one event takes place, then another, then another. Something happened before. Something is happening now. And (we assume) something else will happen in the future.

According to Zen and Quantum Mechanics, the linear, dualistic evolution of time is a construct of this world. Move beyond this world and time as we know it changes form. It ceases to exist. We enter a state of timelessness where there is no more dualism - the past, the present, and the future are all one and the same. Before and after are just two sides of a single coin. In this current world, with these conscious minds, we see the two sides. In the unified mind, we see only the coin - past, present, and future all merge into one.

This concept boggles the senses, which is why Zen masters prefer not to describe enlightenment: there is no way to do it. The human mind cannot conceive of the reality beyond this world. It can't conceive of a fourth dimension and it cannot understand existence without a linear, dualistic progression of time.

We get a glimpse into the unreality of time in this current existence when we look at its relativity. When you do things you like, time seems to pass quickly. When you do things you don't like, it passes slowly. In fact, according to Einstein's theories of relativity, events that occur at one speed for one observer can actually occur at a different speed for another observer, even though both observers are experiencing the same event. We all have a different perception of time, and that perception is our reality for us. Therefore, our realities are relative as well, subjective. The unified mind, though, is objective. And that is the goal of Zen.

Time is another illusion of this world, though a very persistent one indeed. It is simply our perception of change. In this world, change is constant, and so, too, is time. In the unified mind, all simply is. There is no movement. No change. No time. It is the great "I am". It simply exists.

> *"If nothing happened, if nothing changed, time would stop. For time is nothing but change. It is change we see occurring all around us, not time. In fact, time doesn't exist."*
> -Julian Barbour

50

"Do not grow old, no matter how long you live. Never cease to stand like curious children before the Great Mystery into which we were born."

The Christian Bible tells us that we are "awfully and wonderfully created".

Zen masters, Buddhist monks and other spiritual greats have likewise gone on and on about the glory of existence as they have experienced it once they reached enlightenment.

Einstein seems to be testifying to the wonder of life in the same manner as they have. He touched the mystery and has lived in awe ever since. It has made him as if a child, gawking at the Great Mystery before him.

So often, the mystery of life is forgotten. It is unseen. We live in regret of the past and fear of the future to the point that the living moment before us is lost. The most religious among us often see this world as if but a dead carcass - one to be shunned and disliked. Their mind is set on the future glory of paradise, as they believe they have been promised in scripture. In the process, they miss the Great Mystery standing presently before them right here and now.

What Einstein and the Zen masters are trying to tell us is that Heaven is, right now, as we speak, staring us right in the face, and it is beyond all we could ever imagine, if we had but the eyes to perceive it. To do so we must be like a child, devoid of ego and judgment, devoid of past regrets and future fears, experiencing each moment as if it were the first. We must remain childlike in this manner our entire lives if we are to remain open to the Soul of the Universe appearing before us.

"Ego is like dust in the eyes," said the Buddha. "Without clearing the dust, we can't see anything clearly. So clear the ego and see the world."

"Zen is to have the heart and soul of a little child."
-Takuan Soho

51

"I believe in Spinoza's God who reveals himself in the orderly harmony of what exists, not in a God who concerns himself with the fates and actions of human beings."

&

"I don't try to imagine a personal God; it suffices to stand in awe at the structure of the world, insofar as it allows our inadequate senses to appreciate it."

This point has been touched on repeatedly. Einstein found God in the unerring precision and complex vastness of the universe. Mother Nature, the working of the universe, was proof of a vast intelligence beyond the weak and frail human mind. We can scarcely understand the world around us, much less the intelligence that creates and controls it.

Spinoza, like the Zen masters, takes a similar view. God is not a gigantic person, complete with human wants and needs and desires, who concerns himself with the day-to-day activities of his favorites. For them, God is a living energy, a living intelligence, consciousness itself, that creates and runs this world continually.

"Whatever is," says Spinoza, "is in God, and without God, nothing can be or can be conceived."

Zen masters concur but in their own language. Lao Tzu, writer of the "Tao Te Ching", taught that this world is but the division of the one, seen through the lens of duality. His teachings were adopted into Ch'an, which was the start of Zen in China. (Buddhism spread to China and was mixed with Taoism, at which point it was called Ch'an. Ch'an spread to Japan, at which point it was named Zen.) "Out of the one," Lao Tzu says, and I am paraphrasing, "came the two. From the two came all other things." In summary, and in western verbiage, God is the laws of this world and God is the spark of life within all beings. God is the inanimate object, the atoms that create the inanimate object, as well as the energy that forms the atoms that create the inanimate object. God is all of it—the laws and the beings constrained by the laws. All that exists is the one, just in different forms.

Jesus said, "The kingdom of God is inside you and all around you, not in mansions of wood and stone. Split a piece of wood and I am there. Lift a stone and you will find me there."

Willy Wonka said, "If you want to view paradise, simply look around and view it."

Yet because Einstein and the others do not believe in the personified deities of the masses, they are often considered atheists.

> *"My atheism, like that of Spinoza, is true piety towards the universe and denies only gods, fashioned by men in their own image, to be servants of their human interests."*
> "George Santayana

52

"I think ninety-nine times and find nothing. I stop thinking, swim in the silence, and the truth comes to me."

The conscious, analytical, intellectual mind is restricted to this world. It is a product of our genetics mixed with our life experiences and learnings. It is a tool to help us navigate and survive in this world, yet it is limited by the knowledge of this world. To bring something new forth, it must come from a different level of mind.

The unified mind is the world of intuition and imagination. It is the cauldron of possibilities. When we guide our intention on that which we want to bring forth, and think on it, we are setting a goal that both our conscious and unified minds are directed to solve. But to bring something new forth, the conscious mind is inadequate.

After long periods of contemplation, the conscious mind tires and the intuitive magic can come forth.

Most writers say their ideas come "out of the blue", often during sleep when the conscious mind is resting. Artists say the same. We all have this experience. How many times have you sought a solution that eluded you, only to have it come "from nowhere" once you quit thinking about it. This is the unified mind in action, once the ego has given up. The idea has come from the silent source of all imagination.

In Zen, you are seeking to intentionally seek this source. To live from it permanently. Then you live from a level of peace and obtain a knowledge that is not limited to the intellectual mind.

> *"We shape clay into a pot, but it's the emptiness inside that holds whatever we want. We hammer wood for a house, but it's the inner space that makes it livable. We work with being, but non-being is what we use. Existence creates benefit. Emptiness creates usefulness."*
> -Lao Tzu

53

"Behind all the discernible laws and connections, there remains something subtle, intangible and inexplicable. Veneration for this force is my religion. To that extent, I am in point of fact, religious."

&

"Everyone who is seriously involved in the pursuit of science becomes convinced that a spirit is manifest in the laws of the universe – a spirit vastly superior to that of man."

&

"In this way the pursuit of science leads to a religious feeling of a special sort, which is surely quite different from the religiosity of someone more naive."

&

"I do not believe in the God of theology who rewards good and punishes evil. My God created laws that take care of that. His universe is not ruled by wishful thinking, but by immutable laws."

The first quote could literally have come from a Zen book (or a Star Wars movie). The others back up his assertion in his own, scientific understanding.

Einstein is once again saying that he is religious, but not in the traditional sense. He doesn't believe in a personified God made into human form with human motivations. Instead, like the Zen master or Buddhist adherent, Einstein is saying that through his studies he has found an ineffable intelligence that can't be understood or directly perceived. He can't sense it's presence directly, but he has found traces of its actions behind the workings of this world. Whatever it is, it's beyond the frail human mind's ability to fathom.

Veneration for this force is his religion. It's the same power that is personified by other religions, he simply believes that personifying this force is a crude, immature attempt to mold this power into what we want it to be, and to use it for our own personal gain. As Gandhi once said, "God has no religion."

This falls directly in line with Zen teachings. What we see, they tell us, is but an echo. What we don't see is the source from which the echo emanates. Sincere study of the echo eventually leads you to a conviction of a source. Find a way to move beyond the echo and the source becomes apparent.

There is no way to understand the source though, not in the intellectual, analytical way. But you can experience it. You can live within it.

You can't bend it to your personal needs, as we all wish to do. It doesn't have human motivations. It is beyond them. It just is what it is, and if you join it, you will forget your human motivations as well. Do this and all suffering will cease to exist, for your ego will cease to exist. You will no longer be who you thought you were, you will have become a part of the greater whole.

Our egos fear such a thing. It thinks this would mean the death of us. But it doesn't. It means the expansion of what we think we are.

> *"The Force is created by all living things.*
> *It surrounds us and penetrates us.*
> *It binds the galaxy together."*
> -Star Wars

54

"*I am not an Atheist. I do not know if I can define myself as a Pantheist.* The problem involved is too vast for our limited minds. May I not reply with a parable? The human mind, no matter how highly trained, cannot grasp the universe. We are in the position of a little child, entering a huge library whose walls are covered to the ceiling with books in many different tongues. The child knows that someone must have written those books. It does not know who or how. It does not understand the languages in which they are written. The child notes a definite plan in the arrangement of the books, a mysterious order, which it does not comprehend, but only dimly suspects. That, it seems to me, is the attitude of the human mind, even the greatest and most cultured, toward God. We see a universe marvelously arranged, obeying certain laws, but we understand *the laws only dimly. Our limited minds cannot grasp the mysterious force that sways the constellations."*

&

"My religion consists of a humble admiration of the illimitable superior spirit who reveals itself in the slight details we are able to perceive with our frail and feeble mind."

Taoists explain this concept best, in my opinion.
 I am paraphrasing, and explaining in a Western vernacular, but, the "Tao Te Ching" says, "It has no name and it can't be described, yet it is the eternal source of all that we see manifested before us. We give it names and we give it descriptions and motivations and favorites, yet that is our doing.
 "We get caught up so much in appearances that we miss the source, yet both the appearances and the source are one and the same. This is a mystery unfathomable to our human minds, but one that exists nonetheless."

> *"It doesn't take sides - it creates both the good and the bad. It is like an infinite lump of clay, having no form but capable of taking any form. The more you use it the more there is to use. The more you try to understand it, the more it eludes you."*
> -The Tao Te Ching, (my interpretation)

CONSIDER READING NEXT

- "The Tao Te Ching 201" by Matthew S. Barnes.

Matthew's "Zennish Series" books can be read in any order, but Matthew meant for them to be read in the following order:

- Tao Te Ching 101
- Albert Einstein, Zen Master
- Tao Te Ching 201
- Jesus Christ, Zen Master

Or consider the Egyptian Enlightenment Series:

- The Emerald Tablet 101
- The Hermetica 101
- The Kybalion 101
- Bhagavad Gita 101

Or even one of MS Barnes' novels:

- Folie¿
- Meet Frank King

*Be warned that Matthew's novels are not the same as his spiritual works, though they do dive heavily into the power of the mind.

LETTER FROM THE AUTHOR

Dear Reader,

Thank you for reading my book! You've made my day!

I would very much like to know what you thought of my book and why. If you have the time, please leave me a review on Amazon letting me know your thoughts. Remember that the number of reviews a book gets and the number of stars a book gets can make or break your book on Amazon, so please be kind.

If you have any questions or comments feel free to email me at Dr.MatthewBarnes12@gmail.com. I promise I will try to respond.

Thank you for spending time with me!

Matthew Barnes

AUTHOR BIO

Matthew Barnes is an avid learner who spent his early years in North Carolina. During college, he experienced a stint with depression which led him to the works of the Eastern philosophers. He started writing simplified versions of the books he was inspired by in hopes of making the philosophies more accessible to Western minds.

To check the progress on his other works, go to: amazon.com/author/matthewbarnes

in the LIVING moment.